Gladys in Grammarland
and
Alice in Grammarland

THE COVER OF THE FIRST EDITION OF
GLADYS IN GRAMMARLAND

Gladys in Grammarland

by Audrey Mayhew Allen

ILLUSTRATED BY CLAUDINE

AND

Alice in Grammarland

by Louise Franklin Bache

ILLUSTRATED BY HENRY CLARENCE PITZ

Two educational tales inspired by
Lewis Carroll's Wonderland

evertype
2010

Published by Evertype, Cnoc Sceichín, Leac an Anfa, Cathair na Mart, Co. Mhaigh Eo, Éire. *www.evertype.com*.

Gladys in Grammarland
First edition Westminster: Roxurghe Press, ca. 1897.

Alice in Grammarland
First edition Washington, DC: American Red Cross, 1923.

A catalogue record for this book is available from the British Library.

ISBN-10 1-904808-57-3
ISBN-13 978-1-904808-57-2

Typeset in De Vinne Text, Mona Lisa, ENGRAVERS' ROMAN, and *Liberty* by Michael Everson.

Edited by Michael Everson.

Illustrations to *Gladys in Grammarland*: Claudine, ca. 1897.
Illustrations to *Alice in Grammarland*: Henry Clarence Pitz, 1923.

Cover: Michael Everson.

Printed by LightningSource.

Foreword

*T*he two tales in this book are not related to one another, though both are responses to Lewis Carroll's *Wonderland*, and both are somewhat didactic in nature.

Audrey Mayhew Allen was born in 1870, and so was about 27 years of age when she wrote *Gladys in Grammarland*. The edition of *Gladys* itself gives no information about her, but notes in a review called *Literary World*, serialized in the New Zealand publication *Otago Witness*[1], is quite informative:

> Miss Audrey Mayhew Allen, whose new book for young readers, *Gladys in Grammar Land*, is just published by the Roxburghe Press, with droll illustrations by an artist who chooses to remain veiled as "Claudine", comes of a good literary stock. She is a granddaughter of the late Henry Mayhew, author of *London Labour and the London Poor*, and one of the Brothers Mayhew who together wrote so many laughable stories; and she is also a great-granddaughter of Douglas Jerrold. It is a curious circumstance that not only the two authors named, but also her paternal grandfather, Joseph Allen, were all intimately concerned in the launching of *Punch* upon his prosperous career. Miss Allen has for some time contributed stories for children and

1 Dunedin: Issue 2269, 26 August 1879, p. 46

other fiction to various periodicals, but *Gladys in Grammar Land* is, we (*Literary World*) believe, her first book.

No references to specific stories Audrey Allen wrote in the "various periodicals" have come to light—and only a few personal details have. In 1898 Audrey Allen married Harold Hillyard Hampson at St Pancras. They had one son, Philip Harold. The UK National Archives hold a record indicating that Audrey Mayhew Hampson petitioned for divorce from Harold in 1908.

Another review was published in the *The Literary World*[2]:

> Despite the palpable imitation in the title of Audrey Mayhew Allen's *Gladys in Grammarland* there is a good deal of originality in the substance of the book itself, which is written to engage the sensibilities of girls at school, just beginning to struggle with the intricacies of English Grammar, and to help them in their endeavors to differentiate and regulate the Parts of Speech. Gladys falls asleep over her lesson, and is caught away by a Verb and introduced to another and strange world people by Parts of Speech, where Verbs are attended by Adverbs, and Nouns by Pronouns, and where everything so disorderly in books is as orderly as can be, and Adjectives and all the rest march in battle array. An artist signing herself "Claudine" has cleverly illustrated the text, and the pretty quarto is obviously intended for the holiday season, though late in reaching us from its London publisher. [The Roxburghe Press. 3s.6d.]

About "Claudine", the illustrator to *Gladys in Grammarland*, I have been able to find nothing.

The charming *Alice in Grammarland* was written as a play for "Better Speech Week", 5–8 November 1923, and "American Education Week", 18–24 November 1923, and was published in *Junior Red Cross News* in that month

---

2 Anonymous. 1898. "Gladys in Grammarland", in *The Literary World: a Monthly Review of Current Literature* 29(4): 62. (19 February 1898)

and year. Louise Franklin Bache wrote several plays for the *Junior Red Cross News*, and later published a book *Health Education in an American City*.

On "The Teacher's Page", a supplement to the *Junior Red Cross News*, Elizabeth D. Fisher offered the following suggestions about the play:

> Why not let the play spirit of "Alice in Grammarland" linger in your schoolroom and brighten a little some of the routine? What fun your children may have in making a list of offences in English for which the King, Queen, and Jury in Grammarland would order "heads off!" Why not begin this "heads off" list and let it grow as time goes on—did I say grow? Yes, grow and also die. As apparent errors are heard, tried in the Court of the English class and condemned, they are added to the list. As the entire class works together at the execution, certain errors are heard no more and stricken from the list—they have been beheaded.

I'm not sure how popular such a grim approach to grammar correction would be nowadays, but I thought I'd include Fisher's note here as it is part of the history of the story.

Henry Clarence Pitz (1895–1976) of Philadelphia was a painter and illustrator of some renown, who contributed illustrations to numerous magazines and to more than 160 books.

In preparing both of these texts, I have continued my convention of normalizing to Oxford spelling and updating some of the punctuation in light of modern preferences. In *Gladys* I preferred the more modern "quit" to "quitted", "curtsey" to "courtesy", and twice where Gladys was referred to as a "wise little woman" and a "brave little woman" I altered "woman" to "girl", since in reading I wondered if an older person had suddenly entered the tale. In *Alice*, I have also modernized "nick-nack" to "knick-knack", "fidgetting" to "fidgeting", and "spikey" to "spiky". In one place in *Alice*, the White Rabbit uses the word "irrevelant", which I have corrected as a typo for "irrelevant" (p. 72). But I am not sure it wasn't intentional.

As usual, I have indulged in applying Carroll's preference for the spellings "ca'n't" and "sha'n't" and "wo'n't", and set the book in the style inspired by Martin Gardiner's *Annotated Alice*.

Michael Everson
Westport, 21 September 2010

Bache, Louise Franklin. 1923. "Alice in Grammarland", in *Junior Red Cross News*, Volume 5, No. 3, November 1923. pp. 38–40. Illustrated by Henry C. Pitz.

Bache, Louise Franklin. 1924. "Peter Pan's Spring Housecleaning", in *Junior Red Cross News*, Volume 5, No. 5, January 1924. pp. 75–77. Illustrated by Henry C. Pitz.

Bache, Louise Franklin. 1924. "Knights and Ladies of the Great Adventure: A Pageant of the Red Cross", in *Junior Red Cross News*, Volume 5, No. 6, February 1924. pp. 83–85. Illustrated by Henry C. Pitz.

Bache, Louise Franklin. 1924. "National Fete Days the World Around: A Festival", in *Junior Red Cross News*, Volume 5, No. 8, April 1924. pp. 123–125. Illustrated by Henry C. Pitz.

Bache, Louise Franklin. 1934. *Health Education in an American City: An Account of a Five-year Program in Syracuse*. New York, Doubleday, Doran, and Company.

Pitz, Henry Clarence. 1963. *Illustrating Children's Books: History, Technique, Production*. New York: Watson-Guptill, 1963.

Contents

GLADYS IN GRAMMARLAND *3*
I. HOW GLADYS WENT TO GRAMMARLAND *5*
II. HOW GLADYS MET SOME VERBS *15*
III. HOW GLADYS WENT TO COURT *26*
IV. HOW GLADYS WAS PUT IN PRISON *37*
V. HOW GLADYS WENT TO WAR *52*

ALICE IN GRAMMARLAND *61*
PROLOGUE *63*
ACT I *66*
EPILOGUE *73*

Gladys in Grammarland

BY

A U D R E Y   M A Y H E W   A L L E N

I L L U S T R A T E D   B Y
C L A U D I N E

How Gladys went to Grammarland

She was fast falling asleep over her parts of speech. "A noun is the name for a thing. (Horrid stuff!) A noun is the name for a thing. A noun—(oh, dear!) is the—is the—name—is the—"

Poor little Gladys! She had been kept in again. It was always so on grammar afternoons. "Sums were not half so bad," reflected the little girl, "for at least they did sometimes come right; there were interesting parts in Geography and History (not counting dates!), and even Languages might be made pleasant with the rules left out. But Grammar was hopeless!" decided Gladys as she sat with bent, weary head; her tears falling one by one upon the open page of her book, making little puddles and rivulets of the blots there.

Outside in the sunshine the children laughed and chattered merrily upon their homeward way. The earth was bathed in a golden radiance; birds were singing in the trees; rustling leaves murmured to the whispering grass.

Were not those fairy voices inviting Gladys out into the sunshine?

Through the open windows a scent of roses was borne upon the soft little evening breeze. The pretty blossoms were pressing their rosy faces close to the panes. Were not the fairies nodding and dancing there in their sunlit bowers? Within the dusty schoolroom all was silent and dull. The inkspots on Gladys' book and on desks, forms and floor, seemed to form themselves into black faces which grinned at her. The Parts of Speech danced before her eyes, taking the shapes of dark Imps all bent on tormenting her and making her—feel—so—sle–e–py! Gladys' rosy mouth had formed itself into a pout; her eyelids dropped; her tangled curls swept over the table; five inky fingers were soon nestling under a chubby chin.

But she had scarcely closed her eyes for a minute when— poor child!—there was somebody shouting close to her ear: "Come, hurry up!"

"It's no use," murmured Gladys, stifling a yawn. "I *ca'n't* learn it!"

She sat up, nevertheless, and tried to push the odd little man away.

He was a very odd little man. Gladys could not remember having seen him before; but then she felt too sleepy to think. It was unkind of him to bother her just now.

Somebody was pulling Gladys' hair! At that she fairly bounded from her seat. Up flew the grammar-book into the air (where it somehow disappeared mysteriously!), and over rolled the inkpot, which fell with a crash to the floor.

Seated in the middle of the dark pool on the boards was the same odd little man, his legs crossed comfortably. He wore a costume of white foolscap paper cut into points, whilst his crimson stockings reminded Gladys of the material which covered her grammar-book. (But that was nonsense, of course! Gladys must be dreaming.)

"Come, hurry up, do!" repeated the gentleman in the ink puddle. "They're all waiting for us. How do you prefer to travel?"

"Please, I don't understand—and—and please *who are you?*"

"Come, shall we ride, walk, float, fly, swim, dance, caper, scuttle, trip, hop, skip, or jump?"

"Oh, just as you please," answered Gladys with some surprise.

"All's the same to me. I can do anything. I am a *Verb*."

"A what?" cried the little girl, her blue eyes growing big and round with wonder.

"Verb. To Fetch at your service."

Gladys said "Oh!" and stared with all her might.

"You don't understand? Well, it's high time you did. Come along."

"But—where?" enquired Gladys' shrinking away from the monkey-like hand which the Imp stretched out towards her.

"You'll see when you get there." The creature grinned from ear to ear. "*They'll* teach you *there*, ha! ha!"

The child began to look frightened.

"I sha'n't go! " she affirmed stoutly.

"My business is to *Fetch*. Choose your own way, but fetched you shall and must be, whether you like it or no! So make up your mind: will you ride, walk, float, fly, swim, dance, caper, scuttle—"

"You must be active!" laughed Gladys, her fears almost dispelled by the absurdity of the notion.

The Imp opened wide his goggle eyes.

"Why of course I am an *Active* Verb. Don't you know that?"

Gladys blushed and looked foolish.

"I think I should like to fly," she suggested modestly, thinking that there would be, at least, some novelty in that mode of travelling.

"Hey Presto!" Bang! Up they flew like a couple of corks from soda water bottles.

Next moment they were lightly skimming over the housetops.

"Now this—is delightful!" declared Gladys breathlessly. "If—only—it—will—last!"

Afterwards it occurred to her that she ought to have felt more surprised; but at the time it all seemed quite natural. Whether they had quit the schoolroom by means of a window, or by shooting up the chimney, or by crashing through the ceilings of two storeys and out again through the roof, must remain for ever a mystery.

"Where are we going?" she ventured to enquire, as they sped like birds above the topmost branches of a broad forest.

The Imp grinned.

"To *Grammarland*."

"I don't—want—to—go—*there!*" Gladys gasped. No notice whatever was taken of her statement.

Higher and higher they mounted. The schoolhouse, left far behind, appeared like a tiny white speck upon the horizon; whilst Gladys' pretty home nestling amongst trees was completely lost to sight. Up—up—over the hills! and on—on—across rivers, fields, and lakes they flew, whilst the wind whistled in their ears, spreading out Gladys' long hair behind her like a golden cloud. The child was beginning to feel very frightened. Her poor little heart beat pit-a-pat; her breath came and went in sobbing gasps, and her lips were quivering with the brave effort she made not to cry. Then suddenly they paused upon a mountain top.

It had grown dark. Clouds, black as ink, had risen with extraordinary rapidity all over the sky, so that the cheerful rays from the setting sun were completely blotted out. How very strange that those gigantic cloud-shapes should at this moment remind Gladys of certain ugly blots upon the fair pages of her grammar-book!

What a great, bare, dreary-looking mountain it was! The ground at her feet was scored with numberless lines and ciphers, and furrowed with all sorts of strange impressions. Sluggish rivers of an inky substance trickled down the white parchment slopes and were lost to sight in a plain of broken slates below. Gladys shivered.

Taking all these remarkable features into consideration, it did not seem surprising that in front of a hollow upon the mountain's side, there should be a door made of cardboard and covered with faded crimson paper. Across the centre was written in bold black type:

"ENGLISH GRAMMAR."

Gladys had a vague idea that she had seen something of this kind before—somewhere!

Quite suddenly the little man disappeared.

Whilst wondering what could have become of him, and vaguely searching the door over for a keyhole or crack through which he might have passed, Gladys heard a voice speaking sharply upon the other side:

"Lazy girl! Open your book instantly!"

She started violently (the tones sounded so like her schoolmistress's voice!) and, pulling at the sides of the door with all her might, Gladys found that it opened quite easily, like the leaves of a book.

Inside she discovered—not her schoolmistress (that was a relief!) but a long empty passage, the walls of which were composed of thin yellowish paper, flecked here and there with what looked like dirty finger marks.

The first thing that met her eye was:—

"Well—I never!" exclaimed Gladys. "How did *that* get there?"

At the end of a long dreary stretch of corridor she came upon three small letters huddled together in a corner and looking very forlorn:

"P.T.O."

"That means 'Please turn over'," the wise little girl explained to herself. "How polite we are!"

And straightway she turned over a new leaf.

Next moment she came into collision with a long table, and in trying to save herself, tripped up and scattered the contents. The whole alphabet came rattling down upon her as she fell. Gladys—poor child!—was almost buried in the ruins.

Struggling to her feet she stood looking down with an expression of dismay upon the havoc she had wrought. There was nothing for it but to run away, which Gladys did in guilty terror, never stopping to look behind at the broken *Table of Contents*.

In her rapid flight she fled up passages, down passages, and round corners, with eyes closed to the various announcements with which the walls fairly bristled.

At last she paused for breath in a very dirty and dilapidated place, at the other end of which a notice board met her eye.

"Trespassers will be prosecuted, I suppose?" thought Gladys, and felt half inclined to close that leaf and run away again. She plucked up courage, however, and walked slowly on, thinking all the time how nice these white walls *might* have looked if not so dirty, jagged, and torn.

On arriving at the blackboard, this is what Gladys read:

PARTS OF SPEECH.

1. The Noun.   2. The Adjective.

3. The Pronoun.   4. The Adverb.

5. The Verb.

6. The Preposition.   7. The Conjunction.

8. The Interjection.

Gladys tried to remember where she had seen this sort of notice before.

However, she did not trouble her head with much thinking, being anxious to get further on. But the blackboard slid down from its easel like a live thing and completely blocked up the way.

"It's bewitched!" exclaimed Gladys, and a little thrill of delight at this part of the business mingled with her natural astonishment and terror.

Whilst she stood still wondering what on earth to do next, her schoolmistress's sharp voice, which she had heard before, demanded from the other side of the board "Can you say them?"

"Say what?" enquired the child with a jump.

"Your Parts of Speech?"

"Oh, bother! " said Gladys.

All was silent. She beat against the blackboard with her hands, but it stood firm.

Now Gladys was really curious to take a peep at what might be on the other side. Accordingly, after a few moments' poutings and wrigglings, she made up her mind.

She read the notice over two or three times; closed her eyes, put her hands behind her back, and gabbled off the eight Parts of Speech without stopping.

"BANG!"

Up jumped the blackboard, and Gladys peering through the easel's legs, at the same moment exclaimed:

"How funny!"

CHAPTER II

How Gladys met some Verbs

*I*t certainly was an odd sight. Gladys found herself looking down upon a village. Was it a village?

There did not appear to be anyone about, so the child screwed up courage enough to squeeze her body through the aperture, and to descend. This she accomplished by placing her little toes into the notches used for supporting the easel's pegs, and clambering down like a monkey. It was so funny! Gladys laughed to herself, as she wondered what her schoolmistress would think! Now she passed along the principal streets between rows of books placed on end and divided in the middle so as to form little red huts. Very queer they looked with their inkpot chimneys, and reminded one, from a distance, of Indian wigwams.

"They might be very pretty," she reflected, "if only their covers were not peeling off, and their chimneys sending down smoke—I mean ink—all over the walls. The nice white paper curtains too, are all soiled and torn, and really the inhabitants (if there are any) should be made to sweep their doorsteps, for the slate pavement is smothered in dust!"

Truly everything looked dilapidated and dirty, from the ink-dribbling chimney pots to the cracked and dusty pavements. There was a pond at one end of the street with a few worn-out birches planted at intervals along its shores, and a grubby island in the middle. On closer inspection this island proved to be a crumpled pocket handkerchief, which might have been white, once!

With a very grave face indeed, Gladys stooped down, dipped the tip of her finger into the water, and tasted it. It was salt! Salt with the tears she had been shedding over her grammar book!

To light up this mournful scene there was neither sun, moon, nor stars in the blue and white check sky which flapped drearily overhead.

"Why!" Gladys cried aloud with repressed giggles. "It isn't the sky at all. It's only a dirty duster!"

At the sound of her voice a change came over the village. Grammarland awoke!

First of all there was a rustling of leaves, then a fluttering; a scratching of pens, and a screeching of slate pencils. Queer little wizened, impish faces then appeared peeping round the corners of the huts.

Well, Gladys never knew how it happened, but she suddenly found herself in the midst of a busy whirl of little folk. Out they came like bees from a hive, and swarmed over the whole place. None were idle; each one had something *to do*. Some were buying, others selling; some were busy about their little homes; others making pretty knick-knacks with deft fingers; others spinning, others weaving, reaping, heaping, brewing, stewing, draining, training, hoeing, sowing, mowing, tilling, filling. Hither and thither they went, running, walking, jumping, tumbling, stumbling, climbing, sliding, slipping,

16

tripping, skipping, flying, swimming, dancing, prancing, glancing, turning. And all at the same time: talking, laughing, crying, wrangling, jangling, shouting, whispering, yelling, blustering, and flustering; their little black and white legs flying right and left, and their busy tongues keeping pace with the confusion of their movements!

In the midst of all this turmoil stood Gladys, eyes and mouth wide open with astonishment.

Ah, there was that odd little man again!

Afterwards, Gladys could never explain how, with his red legs and black and white hood and cape, his queer little wizened face, long nose and pointed ears, she managed to distinguish her odd friend from his fellows.

Perhaps it was by the expression of his face that she recognized him, for all these Imps had different expressions. Quite unabashed, Gladys caught the active little fellow by one of his tiny, flying legs and drew him to her side. He did not appear to be in the least put out by this unceremonious proceeding.

"Why did you run away from me, little Imp?" she whispered reprovingly. "I have half a mind to box your ears." (No one could have been more astonished than Gladys was at her own daring.) "Now tell me, you horrid little thing! What am I supposed to do in this odd place, and amongst all these odd people?"

The creature grinned from ear to ear. It was a wonder that his mouth did not split.

"Have you seen the King?"

"No, but I should like to very much if you will guide me to where he lives."

"Then you must ask To Guide. I am only To Fetch."

With that the creature wriggled from Gladys' grasp, and in the winking of an eyelash, was gone.

"Well, I do call that cool!" cried our little girl. "The disagreeable thing! I wish I *had* boxed his ears."

Another little wizened face now appeared at her elbow.

"I am To Guide. What is your will?"

"Oh, please, I only want to find—"

"Why not have said so at once? To Find!" shouted the Imp, and darted off as another black and white fellow came running up.

Gladys stood in despair.

"Oh, dear! Oh, dear!" she sighed. "I don't understand. If only somebody would explain!"

"I am To Explain," replied a kind little voice. Gladys turning, beheld a pair of wise, bright eyes, which glanced shrewdly from under their owner's high pointed cap.

"We are *Verbs*, and this is Grammarland. We are *active* little folk, always ready *to do* anything for anybody, though we have our *moods*, which, at times you may find rather troublesome. Although we all appear to be alike, there are a great many classes into which we are divided—for instance, look at those *Strong Verbs* who behave as if the whole of

Grammarland belonged to them. What airs they give themselves because they are able to change their vowels! What good do they gain by it? It only makes children hate them—hard little things! Now we *Weak Verbs*, content to form our past tenses with '*ed*' or '*d*' or '*t*', are easier to get on with, of course!"

"Yes, but what about the King?" interrupted eager little Gladys.

"We have two—King *Common Noun* and King *Proper Noun*; and as each is on the point of making war against the other, it would be better to decide at once whose part you are going to take."

"Very well," said our little maid from school. "Tell me, what they are both like?"

"King Proper Noun is a high and mighty personage who spells his name with a capital letter, and chooses to be considered distinct and separate from everything. Now King Proper Noun looks down upon King Common Noun, a jolly, good-natured soul who is ready to embrace all things, great and small. But matters have come to a crisis between the two, and war has been declared throughout the length and breadth of Grammarland. Therefore say which of these kings do you favour? For let me explain, a great deal depends on *you*!"

"On *me*?" Gladys burst into a merry peal of laughter. "Oh, what nonsense!"

She must have offended the manikin, for he shrank away and left her.

"Which of these two kings do you favour?" repeated another verb, whose name was To Repeat.

"Well, I think King Common Noun must be the *goodest* person of the two," decided Gladys.

Here a sort of shiver passed over the realm of Grammarland. All the little Imps stopped in their various occupations and looked grieved. The little huts rocked as if there was an earthquake, whilst out from one rushed a flying figure with fingers to its ears, and horrified face. It fled shrieking up the street.

"What *have* I done? " cried Gladys, feeling terrified, as well she might.

"It was the Adjective Good," exclaimed a reproachful chorus in low tones.

A small, severe Imp stepped forward from the crowd.

"I am To Correct," he said, casting an awful glance at Gladys. "*Best*', not 'goodest'."

"Because," added To Explain, suddenly putting in an appearance again, "there are some Adjectives which form their Degrees of Comparison by changing their root. But you are using the wrong degree altogether. You should have said the *better* person of the two—that's comparative. You must be careful of this, or you are bound to get into trouble."

Gladys did not understand, but she thought it better not to say anything.

"I should like to be going—" she began.

"Here we *go!*" screeched out a voice like the whistle of a steam engine, and up dashed a figure which seemed to be built on wires. To Go stood before Gladys twisting about, wriggling from one foot to another and making jerky little runs backwards and forwards.

"Ca'n't you keep still a minute?" she suggested impatiently.

"How can he?" exclaimed the chorus, "when To Go is an *active* Verb that ca'n't be made passive?"

"But why not?" questioned Gladys.

They all shivered at her ignorance. To Explain hastened to the rescue.

"*Intransitive* Verbs express an action that does not go beyond the doer."

"Catch an Intransitive verb doing anything except for itself!" put in To Sneer, who had evidently forgotten that he was an Intransitive Verb himself

"*You* ought to know!" said To Jeer.

"Ha! ha!" applauded To Laugh.

"They certainly are selfish," admitted To Explain. Look about you. More than half the verbs in Grammarland are helping one another; the rest are acting for themselves alone. They obey no voice except their own, and what do they gain by it? Nothing but self-gratification. We Transitive Verbs, on the other hand, who suffer our actions to go beyond us, are rewarded. We are allowed *two* voices, Active and Passive. That is only fair. For example—" Here Gladys gave a tremendous yawn. Evidently To Explain was becoming a nuisance. Another Verb stepped forward, pushing To Explain on one side, and cast a reproachful glance at Gladys.

"Oh! " he said, with a shake of his wise little head. "It's all very well for you to shirk your task, but for your own sake allow me to introduce myself: To Remonstrate. After all, we are not so bad, if only you would make up your mind to look at us in a proper light. It is your perverted mind that has clothed us in impish form. You will insist on associating us with bad Adjectives, so what can you expect? Give us a chance—master us. We are ready to become your slaves instead of being your tyrants, if you will only exercise a little common sense. Tackle us with the assistance of the Adverb Sensibly, pay proper attention to Classification and a little respect to Derivation, and then there is nothing we will not do for you."

This speech somewhat impressed Miss Scatterbrain. She did not understand all of it; but turning to the tiny speaker, was about to express her willingness to turn over another new leaf in her grammar, when To Explain suddenly started off again:—

"To begin with, it is necessary to understand that Verbs have *Voice, Mood, Tense, Number*, and *Person*."

Here Gladys lost her temper.

"I daresay! I don't want to know anything more about them. You little wretch! You bore one to death. Be quiet, do!"

Poor To Explain subsided, looking quite crushed. Evidently Gladys was now in a very bad temper, for she next turned sharply upon the active Go, and giving him a poke, cried "Stop fidgeting—do!" The Imp only answered with a naughty grimace, and *went* on just the same.

"You know I want to see the King's palace," continued Gladys, shaking him. Tears of vexation were actually welling up into her pretty blue eyes. The shaking had no effect; in fact the little monster seemed to like it.

"You must put me in the right mood first," he grinned, twisting out of her hands like an eel, and dancing round her. Do what she would, she could not catch him.

"Dunce, dunce, double D!" laughed the wicked sprite.

Gladys burst into angry tears.

"What's the use of—asking you—to do—anything?" she sobbed, "when you still *go* on—"

"That's only *Indicative*," yelled her tormentor. "Try again."

"When you *indicate*, or make an assertion," whispered the persistent little To Explain, coming to the rescue, "you put your verb in the Indicative Mood. He wo'n't go on for that."

"Then what will he go for?" sobbed Gladys. "Oh, you hateful verb!" she continued, turning to her tormentor. "*Are* you *going* to take me to the King's palace or not?"

"Why now you are throwing in a *Present Participle*! What are you about? Ha! ha! What ignorance," and the dancing Imp almost choked himself with laughter.

Poor bewildered little Gladys cried "Oh! Oh!" putting her hands up to her head.

"Don't you see?" whispered To Explain.

"No, I don't!" sobbed Gladys.

Once more she addressed her tormentor.

"Oh! *Go* away—*Go*!" commanded Gladys, "I don't want you at all."

"That's *Imperative*. Very well then, I'm off!" And with an explosive sound, To Go *went*!

Gladys sat down on the ground and fairly cried her eyes out. Oh! She was *so* angry. Heaps of little verbs ran up to comfort her, but she would have nothing to do with them. "I want *To Go*!" she sobbed.

"You silly little girl!" cried the chorus, "And just now you sent him away! But if you only had the sense to put him into the *Infinitive Mood* he would not have gone."

"I told you that he would not do anything to oblige you," observed To Sneer with his nasty smile. "Those irregular Verbs are all alike!"

"Allow me to call To Guide once more," suggested one polite little man, who had hitherto remained in the background. He now came forward and doffed his elfin cap to Gladys with great civility. "I am To Oblige, at your service."

Gladys immediately dried her tears and smiled at the sweet-faced stranger.

"Oh! If you only would—"

"Oblige? With the greatest pleasure." The manikin bowed again.

Gladys then rose to her feet with all the dignity she could muster, made him the sweeping curtsey her dancing mistress had taught her, and said (casting about in her mind for a very big word) "I am *infinitely* obliged to you."

"Bravo!" shouted the chorus so suddenly that Gladys jumped.

"That is distinctly *progressive*," whispered To Explain, patting her shoulder. "Keep it up."

All the Imps were clapping their hands and looking delighted.

To Guide, at the suggestion of To Oblige, now came forward and offered his services for the journey to Court.

"But oh!" gasped Gladys, suddenly recalling the story of Cinderella, "I forgot. What shall I do? Look! I'm so untidy. Oh, dear!"

She glanced down at her shabby schoolroom frock and inky pinafore.

"When we reach the palace," said To Guide, "an Adjective or two will soon put that to rights. But you must not use so many *Interjections*. They are apt to explode."

Now Gladys had not the faintest idea what the Imp meant by this nonsense, but she put her little inky fingers into his, and made ready to start.

"You had better keep me too; you'll want me," whispered a plaintive voice at her side, and looking down she perceived To Explain.

"Oh, very well, come along!" said Gladys, condescendingly; and the three set off together down the long paper street.

CHAPTER III

How Gladys went to Court

*A*ll the streets had names; and the queer part of it all was, that somehow Gladys seemed to be familiar with every one of them.

They passed first over the pond of tears by the Stepping Stones to Knowledge; then down the road to Language, and through Syntax Street into Analysis Square. Such a funny square! No trees, no grass, no flowers! Just

Subject	Predicate	Object
Gladys	learns	her grammar.

"How queer!" thought the little girl.

To Explain produced the key from his pocket, and let them in.

"It is absolutely necessary," he began, as they crossed the great white track, "if you wish to go to Court, that you should understand Analysis."

"Oh, bother!" cried Gladys.

"Nay, listen," advised the gentle To Guide. "You will be grateful to him in the long run, if you do."

"The smallest sentence can be broken up into two parts," proceeded To Explain, "namely, the *Subject* and the *Predicate*. The Subject—"

Here the speaker glanced towards Gladys who was stopping her ears, whereupon he heaved a sigh and dropped the subject.

Next they came to Parsing Grove, which consisted of a double row of ugly black and white sign-posts running in parallel lines on either side of the way.

Naughty Gladys positively declined to walk down Parsing Grove by the side of To Explain. She stood stock still in the middle of the way, refusing to move an inch until that tiresome verb had withdrawn.

"You may join me at the Palace if you like to go by another road," she called out after him, "but I wo'n't be bothered with you all the way there."

There was nothing left to do but for To Explain to take his departure, which he did with many sighs and shakes of the head. But Gladys was not prepared to see To Guide speed after him.

"Come back!" she cried. "I want you."

She ran a little way after him, but was only in time to see four black and white legs vanishing round the corner. It was too bad! Left alone, Gladys retraced her steps to Parsing Grove, and, pausing beneath the first post, read:—

"Lazy"

(Upon the opposite side of the way was written:—)

        Adjective, qualifying Gladys.

(The next sign-post bore her name:—)

  "Gladys" – *Proper Noun*, Nominative Case.

("It gets funnier and funnier, I do declare!" exclaimed the child, and passed on to the third.)

  "Learn"   – *Verb*, Imperative Mood.

(More and mere astonished, she trudged on:—)

  "Your"   – *Pronoun*, Possessive.

(And lastly:—)

  "Lessons"– *Common Noun*, Objective Case, Plural Number.

  "Lazy Gladys learn your lessons!"

Yes, that was what the left hand side sign-posts all said as they pointed with ink-stained fingers at the little dunce.

Gladys could have declared that they were laughing too, with their smudgy mouths, blots of noses, and inky dots of eyes.

Taking to her heels, she ran as fast as ever she could down horrid Parsing Grove, closing her eyes, and stopping up her ears as she went.

Now the road which led up to the King's Palace was called

"ETYMOLOGY."

It was long and steep, and bristling with obstacles, over which Gladys roughly pushed her way, without looking to the right or left, or caring to know what anything meant. In this slipshod way she reached the Royal Palace, which was gilt edged and leather bound, and faced by line upon line of stately pens, their spiky glittering nibs pointed upwards. The outer Courtyard was tiled with brand new slates, and a low fence of sharpened pencils enclosed the whole imposing structure.

The first thing Gladys did was to take a penknife from her pocket and deliberately cut down one or two of the pencils. This difficulty surmounted, she walked boldly up to the high cardboard gates, and thumped at them with repeated blows from her fists.

No one seemed to be in a hurry to open. Then she looked up, and saw written in big letters just above her head:—

"WHAT IS A NOUN?"

"A noun is the name for a thing!" answered Gladys, promptly. Ah! She knew that.

Magical words! The gates flew open and the little scholar found herself in a chequered Courtyard which she seemed to have seen before somewhere.

A blast of paper trumpets greeted Gladys' approach, and in an instant a number of the Royal pages had fluttered out to meet her.

It seemed to the child that thousands upon thousands of little creatures now surrounded her. Some were dressed in rainbow colours, whilst others were *dark* and *ugly*; some were *big*, others *little*, some *fat*, others *thin*, some looked *cross*, others *pleasant*, some *fierce*, others *mild*, *red*, *white*, *blue* and *green*; *tall*, *short*, *broad*, *narrow*, *sour*, *sweet*, *rough*, *gentle*; and *many*, *many*, *many* more besides, they all surrounded Gladys, and all clamoured at once for something which she could not understand.

"Oh, stop! Stop—please!" laughed the child as she stood in the midst of the noisy little creatures with her hands to her ears. "Whatever are you all asking for? Will no one explain?"

Next moment she could have bitten her tongue out; for pushing his way through the crowd towards her came her old friend, or enemy, To Explain, smiling and bland as ever.

"So you are here again!" she exclaimed pettishly, when she could make her voice heard above the din. "Well, since you've come, you may as well tell me what all this noise means!"

"These are '*Adjectives*' and they wish to know how you would like to appear at Court. Will you be—"

The voice of To Explain was drowned in the clamour:

"*Red?*" "*Blue?*" "*White?*" "*Green?*" "*Yellow?*" "*Big?*" "*Little?*" "*Tall?*" "*Short?*" "*Fat?*" "*Thin?*" "*Fair?*" "*Hideous?*"

"Oh dear, oh dear!" cried Gladys in confusion. "What shall I say? I should like to be *beautiful*, of course, like the princess in the fairy tale, and to wear a *long*, *blue* dress with a *red* underskirt, and a *long*, *gauzy* veil!"

Six of the little Imps instantly rushed forward and before Gladys quite knew what had happened, one had perched upon her head, two more upon her shoulders, whilst the fourth, fifth, and sixth disappeared mysteriously amongst the folds of her frock.

Instantly a marvellous transformation took place, and Gladys stood gorgeously arrayed like a princess.

"An Adjective qualifies a Noun," observed To Explain, "that is, shows what the thing is like."

"Come along," said To Guide, suddenly springing up from Goodness-knows-where, like the Imp through the trap door at the Pantomime.

Gladys drew herself up and looked down at him with a dignified air. (Remember she was a princess now.)

"How dared you run away from me just now, Sir?

"You would not be guided," grinned the Imp.

Gathering up the dainty folds of her train, Gladys swept in haughty disdain up the flat ruler steps of the palace, followed and preceded by a number of fluttering pages. Nor was she the only one attended. She noticed that her little companions, To Explain and To Guide, had now each a follower of his own, who trotted by his side and seemed to be pointing out the way.

"Our servants," introduced To Explain. "We call them *Adverbs*, and their duty is to show us *how* to do a thing, *when* to do it, and *where* it should be done. Without them, our actions would seem bare and uninteresting. They follow us about everywhere."

"I did not see them before," said Gladys.

"No doubt you saw, but did not notice them. But you can generally distinguish an Adverb by its ending '*ly*'."

"Do you mean that they are Imps with *tails*?" questioned Princess Gladys, with a giggle.

"Hush! you hurt their feelings. It would be more polite to allude to their *Suffixes*. That one, for instance, who now waits upon me is called Clearly, *Adverb of Manner*. He helps me to explain things."

"Permit me also," struck in the other Verb, "to introduce the Adverb Safely, my especial property."

Both Adverbs bowed to Gladys.

The abode of King Common Noun was more remarkable for oddity than splendour. The walls were of white paper, stamped with short printed sentences. Ceiling and doors of red cardboard, somewhat relieved the monotony of this whiteness, or rather of this dirtiness, for everything (sad to relate!) looked, what Gladys described as "smudgy". Here and there tattered curtains and dog-eared draperies did their best to impart a regal air, but the palace had altogether a dilapidated appearance, as if it might have been clean—once.

Seated side by side at the head of the steps before the door of the throne room, Gladys came across three of the funniest baby Imps she had ever seen! From a distance she fancied the tiny creatures must be blackbeetles, and held her skirts a bit higher in consequence, but as she approached, To Explain informed her "that these were three of the most useful, and at the same time the most tiresome Adjectives in Grammarland."

"What, those babies?" laughed Gladys.

"We call them the triplets, A, and An, and The."

"A and An are only Indefinite Articles," added To Explain contemptuously. "Their brother The is worth them both put together."

"But why do you call them tiresome?" laughed Gladys, half-inclined to pick up one of the funny little things and nurse it.

"Why? Because they are waiting here for King Common Noun to come out in order to tack themselves on to him. Don't touch them! You will never get rid of them if once you do."

"Come along!" broke in To Guide impatiently, "there are dozens more to be seen inside. The silly little things *will* poke their noses everywhere. The worst of it is, they are indispensable to King Common Noun. But he takes care to keep them in their places. They want keeping down, otherwise, babies though they are, they would soon be giving themselves the airs of upstart foreign articles, who want to have *Number*, *Gender*, and *Case* all of their own!"

And now behold King Common Noun, seated in the midst of his dependents upon an inkpot throne, with his Prime Minister, the *Personal Pronoun* It standing at his side.

As Gladys advanced, mincing along in all her finery, with a bland and self-satisfied air; his Majesty cast upon her a look of such deep reproach—nay, disgust, that she stood rooted with astonishment to the pink blotting paper carpet.

Two Verbs, To Surprise and To Arrest, accompanied by the Adverb Suddenly stepped forward, and each laying a hand upon the child, dragged her down to her knees, where she remained in a huddled-up mass before the throne, trembling and wondering what could be the matter. (Poor little Gladys, who had expected to be received as a princess!)

Now the Prime Minister, the Personal Pronoun It, who does duty for King Common Noun, was about to pronounce sentence upon the unfortunate Gladys, when his Majesty suddenly checked him, and turning to her, said in tones of sorrowful enquiry:—

"Why did you spoil our Palace?"

"ME?" gasped the little girl.

Everyone shuddered. The Prime Minister drew himself up with a dignified air.

"*I!*" whispered To Correct frantically in Gladys' ear.

King Common Noun sighed and continued: "You have completely ruined our palace with ink, dirty fingermarks, and rents—our palace that once was so clean, and neat, and firmly bound! Moreover you have insulted Us, by refusing to learn what we could teach you, and many a time have you scratched us through with pens, rubbed us unmercifully with hard india-rubber, until we became quite

faint, and blurred us with idle tears, and now you come here—"

At this point a *violent* Adjective bounded quite unexpectedly upon the throne and whispered something in his Majesty's ear. Whereupon the good-natured face of that Monarch suddenly underwent an alarming change, and raising his voice to a pitch of fury, he continued:—

"You dare to come here, expect us to receive you pleasantly. Away with her! Let her be cast into the dullest schoolroom! There give her ten pages of Syntax to learn, that she may know in future the different peculiarities of the parts of Speech."

A small body of Imperative Verbs at once rushed towards the trembling Gladys.

"*Seize* her!" cried one. "*Drag* her along!" "*Let* us *punish!*"

"Oh, pl–e–a–s–e!" shrieked the little mock princess, "'I will be good."

Too late! She felt a bumping and a thumping as she sank down—down—down into

THE DEEPEST DUNGEON BENEATH THE

CASTLE MOAT.

CHAPTER IV

How Gladys was put in Prison

When at length Gladys ventured to look about her, she uttered a little cry of surprise.

"Why—why—this must be the school-room again!"

She was seated at her own desk upon which lay her grammar, her slate, copy book, and pencil box. All her things were there—but oh! horrible to relate, in every other respect, the room had undergone a terrible change.

In the first place, most of the furniture had been cleared out, little remaining except Gladys' chair, one or two desks, and the blackboard, standing on its three-legged easel against the wall.

Where were the pictures? The hearthrug? Miss Primer's little table, with the bowl of flowers upon it? Things with which that kind mistress loved to adorn the school-room, making it fair and cosy for her little pupils.

The whole place was steeped in gloom. No, no! This could not be the cheerful and bright school-room! Her eyes turned towards the windows or to where the windows should have been, for even they had disappeared. One small aperture alone remained. It was close to the ceiling, cross-barred with iron rulers, and it let in only the faintest glimmer of light; not a glimpse of a golden sunbeam, nor of a green tree-top, nor a vestige of blue sky was to be seen.

Oh, how bitterly poor Gladys cried as she glanced round that awful room. Like Cinderella she was back in her old place again, stripped of her finery—no longer a fairy princess, but a very untidy and grubby little school girl, half frightened out of her wits by the terror of her position.

Steps sounded upon the stone corridor without. A key was fitted into the lock, the ponderous door swung back screeching upon its rusty hinges, and a female jailer appeared.

Next moment Gladys uttered a joyful cry, and stretched out both hands.

"Oh, Miss Primer, *dear* Miss Primer, I am so glad you've come!"

Gladys' schoolmistress set down a loaf and a jug of water in grim silence upon the floor.

"Miss Primer," enquired Gladys, in a tremulous voice, "are you going to let me out of this dreadful place? I will be *so* good."

"Do you know your lesson?" asked a stern voice.

"No–o–o," sobbed Gladys, "that is, not quite all."

"Then," replied Miss Primer in terrible tones, "you will remain here upon bread and water until you do. Kindness is utterly thrown away upon you."

The child glanced timidly into Miss Primer's face. Could this be the kind mistress whose patience and forbearance she had lately taxed beyond limits, this stern individual, with the relentless face and fiery dragon eyes? Gladys had not a word to say. She shivered a little, covered her face with her hands and sobbed.

"In my young days," pursued the lady witheringly, "the Educational System was conducted on quite a different basis. 'Don't Care' was made to care. Nowadays things are far too easy for young people—mistaken kindness! If you are slow to learn, I shall be quick to punish."

Gladys felt as if she had suddenly stepped into a cold bath.

Frowning with lowering brows upon her terrified pupil, the schoolmistress then departed and the heavy door closed behind her with a clang.

Left alone, Gladys was at first too bewildered to think. She got up and ran round her prison, beating her soft little hands against the hard walls. The blackboard grinned at her through the gloom. Yes, there it stood with legs apart and grinning face, wide mouth, big teeth, monster nose, pointed ears. The very face which Gladys had drawn in laughing mood upon the blackboard that afternoon, and hurriedly rubbed out again, now reappeared, clear and white through the gloom to mock at her. Certainly there was nothing left for her to do but return to her desk and learn the ten pages of Syntax.

She groped her way back to her place and shading her poor little throbbing brows with both hands to shut out that laughing face, bent her eyes upon her book.

Syntax teaches us how words are put together in a sentence. It treats of the right use of the parts of speech and their inflexions. This is what she had to learn. How hard the chair felt, and the desk, too, seemed to be bristling with bumps. Gladys ached all over from her head to her toes.

The chief combinations of the Parts of Speech are—

How dark it was! She could scarcely see her book. Oh! What would she not have given now for the companionship of To Explain.

1. A verb and its subject, as, "Time flies."

2. An adjective and its noun, as, "A good man."

A tiny ray of light struggled in through the barred window and fell upon the open book. Dear little moonbeam! Was it a fairy come to comfort her?

3. A verb and its object; as—

"*Gladys learns her lessons,*" suggested a sweet voice close beside her.

Oh, dear little welcome voice! There was To Explain, smiling down at Gladys. And, strange to say, he no longer looked like an Imp. He might have been a fairy, Gladys thought, so bright and clear and shining was his aspect in that dark dungeon. She could have hugged him.

"Oh, you've come at last!" she sobbed. "It *is* kind of you, considering how much I have—s–snub–b–ed you! Oh, stay with me—don't go away!"

The fairy spoke tenderly.

"Of course I will stay with you unless you drive me from you again. You know, Gladys, that To Explain is only too

happy to help you, more especially so, when he is suffered to
tread in the footsteps of his good little brother To Try."

To Explain pointed to the desk. There, just above Gladys'
book, hovered another fairy form. Such a patient, happy face
was his! There were lines upon his little forehead, and
shadows beneath his weary eyes, yet a bright and hopeful
smile curved the fairy's pretty lips.

"Why," said Gladys, " I never saw *you* before!"

"No," was the patient reply, "you never would, but you will
now, wo'n't you Gladys?"

"To work!" interposed To Explain briskly.

And for once Gladys did work.

It seemed as though hours and hours went by whilst the
three pored over their task. With these kind little friends to
help and encourage her, it was not so bad after all, Gladys
thought.

Her prison became more bearable as the light gradually
dawned in upon her. One by one, the morning sunbeams stole
in through dungeon bars and flickered upon the walls. The
mocking face had faded from the blackboard—that *was* a
comfort! How could it remain there when fairy sunbeams
were dancing on the old easel in the morning light?

And now they rested from their labours. How delightful it was to know that there had been "Something attempted—something done!" for once in a way.

"All work and no play will make Gladys a dull girl," said To Explain. "Let's have a game."

Gladys would far rather have been let out of prison first, but she did not like to offend the little fairies.

"It's not a pleasant place for a romp," she suggested however, with a little grimace.

"Who wants to romp? We are not tomboys."

"I have been told that I am one," admitted Gladys, blushing.

"We will teach you a nice instructive game," said To Try, gravely.

"Oh, dear!" thought Gladys despairingly to herself.

"Do you know *How, When, and Where?*"

"Oh, yes!" the little girl was all animation at once. "One person goes out of the room, whilst the rest think of a word. Let me go out first!"

"We don't play like that in Grammarland."

"Then I sha'n't play at all! " pouted Gladys.

"For instance, we will think of the word 'Grammar' itself," went on To Explain blandly, "Now *how* do you like it? Quick! Give us an *Adverb of Manner.*"

But Gladys sulked.

A horrid little green and yellow goblin flew in through the bars of the grating and alighted wriggling in her lap.

"Ugh!" shrieked the child. "Take it away!"

"The Adverb Sulkily," introduced To Explain.

"Oh!" screamed Gladys. "Oh!'"

"Then how *do* you like grammar?"

"I like it—oh!—oh!—*pretty well!*"

"She likes grammar pretty well!" repeated both fairies together, and—hey presto! the adverb Sulkily vanished.

"Now, *when* do you like grammar?"

"Some—sometimes! " faltered Gladys.

"'Sometimes', *Adverb of time.* Right!"

"And *where* do you like it? " pursued her questioner.

"He–e–ere!" wailed the child with a shudder.

"'Here', *Adverb of place.* Right again!"

"That's all!" said To Explain. "Isn't it a nice game?"

"I suppose now," suggested Gladys, drying her tears, "I may come out of prison?"

Her companions looked at one another.

"*You* tell her," said To Explain.

"I'll try."

To Try seated himself cross-legged upon the desk, with his arms folded upon his elfin breast, and his weird little face on a level with the child's own. "You see," he began, "there are conditions." He cleared his throat and proceeded. "The fact is you are in an awkward position, between two stools, as it were." (Gladys looked about her. She would have been grateful for *one* stool to rest her poor aching feet upon!) "Namely King Common Noun and King Proper Noun," added To Explain.

"King Proper Noun is fond of dictating! He will put himself at the head of everything. He even considers King Common Noun has no right to a title at all. That has got to be scratched out of him," continued To Explain, working himself into a great passion. "Yes, scratched out with pens— and knives!"

"It's easy to tell whose side *you* are on," laughed Gladys.

"Of course, I belong to King Common Noun. Don't I explain *things*?"

"Of course. But I should like to know what all this has to do with my being in prison?" sighed the poor forlorn little captive.

"You have fallen into King Common Noun's bad books."

"Well, dear little Fairy, how am I to get out of them?"

Here the two verbs took counsel together in whispers whilst Gladys waited.

At length the verdict was given.

"Attend," said To Try. "There are two conditions: First, you must promise to write at your earliest opportunity a composition of which King Common Noun will take the title."

Inwardly Gladys groaned. Aloud she said meekly, "Very well, I'll try."

Whereupon the fairy suddenly leaning forward, grasped her gently by the shoulders, lifted his little nose high in the air and kissed her!

It nearly took her breath away.

"Secondly," continued To Explain, "you must work your way back into King Common Noun's good books. This must be done at once. Quick! Have you India rubber?"

"Yes," said Gladys opening her pencil box.

"And a pen knife?"

"Yes."

"A needle and cotton?"

"No–o–o—Oh, but wait a minute! Nelly Strange always keeps such things in her desk next to mine. She's so tidy. Yes, here they are."

"Armed with these," cried To Explain, flourishing the implements, "we shall soon clear space. Ha! ha! Come along!"

"But—" began Gladys.

"Leave that Conjunction alone!" shouted To Try so suddenly that she jumped.

The fairies seized her by either hand and drew her rapidly towards the door.

After all it was easy as possible. When they reached the keyhole they just popped through.

They were back in the dirty white corridor again. Alas! In the morning light it looked more dilapidated and crumpled up than ever.

"We've got to patch this place up," said To Try.

"However can we? " asked the child. Visions of painters, whitewashers, and decorators floated through her mind.

To Explain answered by mutely pointing to her knife and India rubber. It was pretty evident that Gladys was expected to do it, for upon the door at the farther end of the corridor a bill had been posted:—

CLOSED FOR ALTERATIONS
AND REPAIRS
By Gladys.

"Perhaps you feel inclined to buy us a new Palace instead," suggested a voice close to her ear. She turned just in time to see that nasty little verb To Sneer running away.

"Buy a new palace for them indeed! The idea!"

There was another horrid little yellow-eyed goblin sitting upon Gladys' shoulder! She made a feeble effort to shake it off, but it stuck to her like a leech.

Then dear little To Try accompanied by his Adverb Again came to her assistance. In a twinkling the goblin was pulled down from his elevated position, and for safety put into Gladys' pocket. His name was Pride.

Meekly taking up her pen-knife; the little girl began to scrape the inkstains from the walls of the corridor. It was no easy task, for the knife was apt to make holes in the thin white paper; but surely good fairies must have been helping her—or was the little knife bewitched? for in a remarkably short space of time the walls began to look fair and white, though a trifle scrubby.

But the next labour was dreadful.

Gladys found herself obliged to go down upon her hands and knees and clean the floor from end to end with India rubber. It was no use crying over it, for her tears rolling down upon the cardboards only made them the more smudgy, and redoubled her task."

But that was not all. There were a number of loose pages fluttering about.

To these Gladys gave chase, and after a heated pursuit, caught them by their dog's ears, and bound them firmly together. The trials she went through before *that* work was accomplished were enough to drive one crazy!

All the pages were numbered; yet they seemed to take a fiendish delight in getting mixed. Hither and thither Gladys rushed, chasing them as they flew before her. Some came out of the conflict terribly torn. Pages 5 and 6 were so ragged and tattered that Gladys blushed for them. When she had collected about a dozen, she set to work, hot and breathless, to sew them together.

How they rustled, flapped, and fluttered, as the sharp little needle pierced their flattened dog's ears, drawing the long cotton after it. In spite of all their struggles and groanings, the operation went on. The difficulty was to arrange them in their right places.

"Ask a conjunction or two to help you," suggested To Try, at this moment when the giant Imp Despair had almost seized Gladys in his painful grasp.

"Yes, we will help you," exclaimed a chorus of little cheery voices, and up ran a party of tiny fellows, amongst which, one labelled And was very conspicuous.

"We Conjunctions *are used for joining together*," said the first one.

"Yes, whenever you are in want of a little sticking paste, we can always supply it " laughed the second.

"But leave But alone—he's dangerous!" a third whispered mysteriously.

Despair was driven away; the brave little girl now went on stitching for dear life, helped by her kind, busy friends.

And now at last the rebellious pages were all drawn up according to their numbers and neatly bound together—1, 2, 3, *and* 4, 5, 6, 7, 8, 9, 10, 11, *and* 12!

"At last! At last!" cried Gladys, jumping to her feet and dancing about. "How nice it all looks; how clean and tidy! I am sure King Common Noun cannot now complain—no! Nor King Proper Noun either!"

Seizing her bundle of captive pages, she walked boldly down the corridor followed by her body-guard of conjunctions, whilst To Try and To Explain brought up the rear.

The door of the throne-room fluttered open to admit the little procession, and Gladys in triumph, knelt and laid her trophies at King Common Noun's feet.

In that proud and happy moment, the dear, insignificant-looking little conjunction And, whose duty was to join together the broken pieces of Grammarland, raised her gently from the ground.

Motioning away the mischief making adjective Angry, who still hovered about his Majesty, also those cruel verbs in their imperative moods, the little fellow placed Gladys' hand within that of the Monarch, and peace was restored.

Glancing up at the wall behind the throne, Gladys saw these words written:—

"Gladys joined by the conjunction And to King Common Noun."

She was wondering how they came there, when a commotion at the other end of the hall attracted her attention. A messenger dashed forward.

"King Proper Noun with a whole volume of words, has stormed the front lines of Grammarland; has spelt his name thereon with a capital letter and already seized and taken a vast number of adjectives!"

King Common Noun leaped from the throne.

Instantly the whole scene became one of active preparation.

Verbs ranged themselves in their tenses assisted by such adverbs as Promptly, Courageously, Obediently.

A great number of *Prepositions* ran about. They were wanted everywhere.

These little Imps, although like the conjunctions, very insignificant-looking, at this crisis proved themselves to be quite important Parts of Speech. Gladys, who had learnt in Syntax that "Prepositions mark the relations between words in a sentence," and had hammered the definition into her head without any idea as to its meaning, now began to form some notion as to its practical sense, as she beheld the Prepositions in Grammarland taking up their positions as sentinels "*in*" the palace, "*at*" the gates, "*outside*" the walls, and "*upon*" the ramparts.

The adjectives completely lost their senses. Poor things! They knew that they would be first to fall captives under the sway of the conquering Proper Noun. So they huddled themselves all together around their sovereign and afforded a most piteous spectacle.

In the midst of the hubbub and confusion King Common Noun raged and blustered like a whirlwind.

"Arms! Arms!" he roared.

"What is all this nonsense about?" enquired Gladys, who alone seemed calm.

It was supporting his Majesty, who had completely broken down.

"Arms! Arms! " sobbed the distracted Monarch. "Have they all gone over to the enemy?"

"This is too absurd for anything!" exclaimed Gladys.

"Yes—Anything!" cried It. "Go fetch any '*thing*' for his Majesty to arm himself with. Only Common objects, mind!"

Gladys rushed off shaking with laughter. She tumbled upon a lot of dustpans, dish covers, and saucepans on her way. How funny that they should be there!

"To be sure they are common objects," she thought. "They will do."

She gathered them up quickly and returned in triumph with them to the King.

King Common Noun revived and assisted by Gladys and It was soon armed at all points.

And now line upon line of glittering Adjectives fell into their places as King Common Noun arrayed in his armour, headed the list with the Prime Minister It at his side.

Three pronouns shrank timidly in the rear. They were poor Relatives, and entirely dependent upon these two mighty personages. Their names are better known as Who, Which, and What.

Verbs in their perfect tenses swelled the vocabulary, rows of modifying Adverbs took up their positions close behind them; whilst numbers of Conjunctions, stationed amongst the Parts of Speech formed, as it were, the links of the army.

"Of course!" reflected Gladys. "For how could a mere muddle of words be arranged so as to form sense without a conjunction or two here and there between?"

From the ramparts she watched the mustering of the troops, and how the whole vocabulary moved on through Grammarland with paper banners waving, burnished pens glittering, and steely pencils pointed in the air.

CHAPTER V

How Gladys went to War

The next thing Gladys remembers is her first sight of King Proper Noun.

By advantage of her superior height she was the first to mark him, advancing at the head of a similar army.

His appearance was most extraordinary! In the first place this monarch seemed to resemble everybody else that Gladys had ever seen.

This sounds vague, but you must ask our little heroine how it was she came to see so many likenesses.

Then, he wore a cloak embroidered with the portraits of the kings and queens of England, also a great many more exalted personages whom Gladys did not recognize. And actually a miniature of Gladys' little self hanging from his neck. Well, it was like his impudence, she thought! The patterns upon his vest looked like a map, whilst rivers with long names wound around his long black and white legs.

Gladys noticed also with dismay that his odd Majesty was accompanied by no less than *seven* Prime Ministers. This was dreadful. What if they should all want to have her arrested? (How there could be seven, and all be *Prime* Ministers did not occur to her! Everything was at odds in Grammarland.)

She was so frightened that, with three bounds she had cleared the ramparts and reached the side of King Common Noun. Stooping down she whispered breathlessly in his Majesty's ear: "Here's King Proper Noun coming along at the head of *seven* Prime Ministers and a much bigger army than your own!"

King Common Noun became a piteous object. It supported him.

"Look here," said Gladys with sudden inspiration. "Go back home and don't be silly. What do you want to fight at all for?"

"What for?" groaned the King. "Miserable child! When the battle is all on your account!"

"Oh, but that's all nonsense, you know," laughed the little girl. "And I'm not a 'miserable child'—I'm Gladys."

"Sh–h–h! For goodness' sake, don't mention *names*! I consider you as a 'child'. That's a common noun. Don't be so proper!"

"I don't know what on earth you are talking about!" Gladys went on laughing.

King Common Noun explained.

"There's some dispute as to your gender. As a matter of fact I suppose you are Feminine. Ask It."

It held its nose in the air. Gladys could have shaken It.

"But in order to come under my rule," continued his Majesty in deeply harassed tones, "you will have to change your gender."

"Well, and so I will," agreed Gladys cheerfully, "if that will satisfy you. I'm sure I don't care which it is."

King Common Noun glanced interrogatively towards It. It's nose was still in the air. It really was very aggravating of It.

"It's an awkward case, isn't It? " whispered the trembling monarch, drawing her hastily to one side. "You see, It very naturally objects to your adopting It's gender."

Gladys sat down on the ground and laughed till she cried. "The whole thing is absurd. Bosh!" she exclaimed loudly.

BANG!

"Oh! what's that?"

"There goes some of our ammunition!" groaned the King. "Why do you meddle with Interjections? You don't understand how to handle them, and then off they go."

Now this conversation took place whilst the two armies were drawing up opposite to each other upon the white paper plain.

A blast of paper trumpets announced that all was in readiness. King Common Noun pulled himself together with a visible effort, though his knees shook.

"Form Sentences!" he shouted; and at once various detachments of words marched towards the enemy's lines.

Gladys read the first sentence.

"A *COMMON NOUN* IS THE NAME
OF EACH INDIVIDUAL IN THE SAME CLASS
OR SORT OF THINGS; as *MAN, CHILD,
BOOK, TREE, HOUSE, CITY,* &c."

Et sat upon the ground with C in front of him, and held his leg in the air.

Gladys never saw such a comic little Imp.

"These foreign conjunctions," whispered To Explain, "are so eccentric!"

At the same time King Proper Noun sent back in defiance:—

"A *PROPER NOUN* IS THE NAME
OF ONLY ONE PERSON OR THING CONSIDERED
INDIVIDUALLY as, *HENRY, LONDON, JUPITER*, &c."

"Yes, those are the words of my grammar book," thought Gladys, "but I never understood them until now."

She made a last appeal to King Common Noun: "Do use a little common sense. Give up the battle. You're bound to get the worst of it. Why, King Proper Noun is big and strong enough to carry off you and your subjects and palace all at once!"

"Never," asserted his Majesty solemnly. "Never! He might up-*root* us; cut us up, make us *compounds*, or scratch us out altogether; but he could never remove our palace for that is *Stationary*!"

With these words he dashed forward to the Frontispiece and made ready for the battle.

At the same moment a Herald advanced from the enemy's lines and shrieked through a long paper trumpet:—

"GLADYS!"

"Me?" cried Gladys with a start.

A shiver ran through the ranks. The Pronouns almost broke down, though the first of the seven recovered sufficiently to gasp:—

"*I!*"

"I," repeated Gladys meekly. "I beg your pardon. I meant 'I'."

"Badly expressed!" remarked King Proper Noun. But the Herald had come to a *Full stop*.

"Go on!" roared his Majesty. "Never mind the punctuation!"

Thus commanded, the Herald made a *dash*—

"*GLADYS—YOU MUST FIGHT UPON OUR SIDE!*"

"I sha'n't! " said Gladys.

The two armies formed Notes of Interrogation (?). The Prime Ministers put their heads together. King Proper Noun took a step forward.

"Ourself," he said with dignity, "as represented by the personal Pronouns, 'I', 'Thou', 'He', 'She', 'We', 'You', and 'They', have decided that Gladys shall fight upon our side."

"I sha'n't do anything of the kind," cried Gladys, astonished at her own boldness.

"Child! Child!" implored King Common Noun, plucking nervously at her sleeve.

"You must fight upon our side!" shouted King Proper Noun, now in a violent passion. "Why, you are a Proper Noun yourself!"

"I'm not."

"You spell your name with a capital letter," roared the King. "There is only *one* Gladys; consequently you are a proper noun and belong to *Me!*"

"I wo'n't be a proper noun," persisted Gladys. The two armies looked at one another and shuddered again and again at her ignorance.

"That settles it then," said King Common Noun, boldly. "The battle cannot proceed. It's clear that '*Gladys*' belongs to your side, but you see '*the child*' refuses to fight for you."

"Why not fight without me?" suggested the mischievous little girl.

"Impossible!" exclaimed King Proper Noun. "The idea is absurd, considering that the battle is all on your account.'"

"On my account? Why, I never heard of such a thing. What have *I* done?"

"You have refused repeatedly to see the distinction between myself and King Common Noun, and it therefore remains for us to show you which is the more important."

"Stuff and nonsense! " cried Gladys loudly.

There was a great explosion like bomb shells. Both armies became paralysed.

"That's as bad as an Interjection," said King Proper Noun, "and if you use Interjections, we shall have to turn you out of Grammarland neck and crop.

"I wo'n't go," was the prompt rejoinder.

The Kings were fairly staggered.

"Come," continued Gladys, still more and more surprised at her own courage. "Why don't you make it up? I *do* understand the difference between you—now! You are *both* very important, and I'm sure," she added, awkwardly framing a soothing little compliment, "that the grammar book could not do without either of you."

Both Kings looked extremely gratified.

They grasped hands. The two armies recovered, and formed Notes of Admiration (! !) opposite to each other. Peace was declared.

Why did Gladys instantly spoil the good effects produced by her words?

Heedless little Gladys! With a burst of laughter she exclaimed suddenly: "After all, what does it matter? You're only a lot of stupid grammar stuff, and I don't care two pins—Oh–h–h!"

BANG!

Another of those terrific explosions!

The two armies rushed furiously at her. Then helter skelter! There was a terrible jumble of Nouns—Pronouns—Verbs—Adjectives—Prepositions—Conjunctions and those dreadful Interjections; much rustling of paper and scratching of pens, scraping of pencils and screeching of slate pencils; followed by a sound like the closing of the leaves of a book; then—Silence.

Gladys awoke!

She sat up and rubbed her eyes! Why, she was back in the school-room again; but this was no dungeon! The grammar book lay under the table, the contents of her pencil box were scattered; and a broken inkpot was the cause of a dark stream upon the floor; otherwise everything looked much the same as usual; with the golden sunlight pouring into the room and all things bright and beautiful outside.

The clock struck five. Steps sounded along the passage outside. It was dear Miss Primer coming to let her out.

Yes, Gladys had evidently been dreaming, but all the same, she knew her lesson perfectly.

Alice in Grammarland

BY
LOUISE FRANKLIN BACHE

ILLUSTRATED BY
HENRY CLARENCE PITZ

CHARACTERS OF THE PLAY

ALICE.

DINAH, a real cat.

THE WHITE RABBIT, herald of the court.

THE QUEEN, author of the grammar book.

THE KING, the Queen's husband.

TWELVE JURORS, animals and birds.

    (*This number may be reduced if desired.*)

THE HATTER.

THE DUCHESS.

TWEEDLEDEE and TWEEDLEDUM.

TWO SOLDIERS.

THE LORD HIGH EXECUTIONER.

THE CLERK OF THE COURT.

Prologue

(*The Prologue may be given in front of stage curtain.*)

ALICE [*enters with cat under one arm and a book of English composition under the other. Advances slowly talking to cat*]: Now, Dinah, there is no use in making a fuss. You are going to study your English lesson whether you wish to or no. Your purrs sound *very* rusty lately. Besides, I have noticed to my great distress that you have fallen into the way of punctuating your sentences with wags of your tail in quite the wrong places. Punctuation marks are precious things. You have to be awfully careful how you scatter them about. There, I do not mean *awfully* but *very* careful, Dinah. Observe the correction, please, and profit by it. [*Advances to centre of stage. Seats herself on ground; opens book; holds it before* DINAH.] Dinah, stop looking around this minute. How can you expect to learn your lesson if you keep your head turning like a windmill? Concentrate, my dear Dinah, concentrate! Perhaps you do not know what concentration means. You don't? Well there is a nice little rule which goes like this—"A new word learned each day will help you express your thoughts in the best and fullest way." Just think, Dinah, of all the wonderful things you could tell me if only you had a larger vocabulary. Hm! You do not wish to learn a new word. Well, I'm truly sorry, Dinah, but one has to do a great many things one doesn't wish to, you know.

RABBIT [*enters in haste without observing* ALICE]: Oh! My ears and whiskers, how dark it is getting! I shall be late at Court.

ALICE: Curious! Curiouser! Curiousest! [*Scrambling to feet.*] No, that is all wrong, Dinah. I mean, curious, more curious, most curious. That is the most curious sight I have ever seen!

RABBIT [*rushes back and forth across stage*]: The Queen, the Queen! Oh, my dear paws! Oh, my fur and whiskers! She'll have me executed as sure as cats are cats.

ALICE: [*intercepts* RABBIT]: I heard you mention a Queen. I'd give anything in the world to see a real Queen.

RABBIT [*stops; looks* ALICE *over; spies cat, shudders; hurries off; speaks over shoulder*]: Your language is wantonly extravagant. However, for your benefit I will say that no one who carries a carnivorous, domesticated quadruped is permitted to gaze at my Queen.

ALICE [*rushes after* RABBIT; *grabs sleeve*]: You use such long words I am not sure that I know what you mean. If you are by any chance speaking of my cat, I can assure you she will not mind being left at home.

RABBIT [*struggling to free himself*]: I speak English. If you cannot apprehend the meaning of my words, whose fault is it? [*Exit* RABBIT.]

ALICE [*slowly*]: I guess he does mean you, Dinah, after all. [*Exit from stage. Voice from off stage*]: Run along! You are excused from your lesson today.

Act I

Scene: Court in Palace of King *and* Queen *of Grammarland. A double throne on raised platform in centre back of stage.* King *and* Queen *are seated on throne. The* King *is judge. He wears crown over wig. Holds book written by* Queen. *The* Queen *wears spectacles, and knits. Two* Soldiers *stand on either side of* King *and* Queen. *The* Lord High Executioner *takes his place on the opposite side from that occupied by the jury.* Jurors *are writing on slates when scene opens. Their slate pencils squeak frequently. The* Clerk of the Court *sits at low table in front of them.* Rabbit *accompanied by* Alice *enters.* Alice *stands by jury box. Every time a pencil squeaks she covers her ears.* Rabbit *bows low before throne.*

KING [*in thundering tones*]: Come to order at once! Herald, read the accusation.

RABBIT [*unrolls scroll; reads*]: "The Queen of Grammarland wrote a book, all on a summer day. The King of Grammarland took that book, and ordered all its rules to obey." [*To* KING]: There are some, your Majesty, who refuse to comply with the royal decree.

KING [*sternly*]: Summon the offenders before me at once!

RABBIT [*blows on trumpet. Two* SOLDIERS *rush down throne steps and out. Return with the* HATTER *as prisoner.* SOLDIERS *take former places.*]: The Hatter, your Majesty.

HATTER [*enters with hat on head, a teacup in one hand, and a piece of bread and butter in the other*]: I beg your pardon, your Majesty, for bringin' these here things with me.

KING [*sternly*]: Remove your hat. Can you not see there are ladies present?

HATTER: Say, listen! The hat ain't mine.

CLERK OF THE COURT: It must have been stolen then. [*To* JURORS]: Write that down. [JURORS *repeat words in chorus. Pencils squeak.*]

HATTER: The hat ain't stole. I'm a hatter, I keep 'em to sell, I ain't got none of my own. I'm an awfully poor man, your Majesty.

CLERK OF THE COURT: I have evidence to prove that the prisoner has his pockets full of gold.

KING: I do not wish your evidence. I judge a man's wealth not by the gold he has in his pockets, but by the words he lets fall from his mouth. Therefore, I agree with the Hatter. He is a poor man—a *very* poor man.

QUEEN [*looking over spectacles*]: The Hatter has never studied my grammar or he would not use incorrect words nor drop letters from his words. I therefore recommend, my dear [*turning to* KING], that he be given the prescribed punishment for such offences.

KING [*nods approval. To* EXECUTIONER]: Off with his head! [EXECUTIONER *grabs* HATTER *roughly. Turns him with face to wall. Resumes his place in court.*]

ALICE [*stamps foot*]: I never heard of anything so absurd in my life. Imagine losing your head because you make mistakes in your English!

QUEEN [*calmly*]: It is not so absurd as it seems, my dear. What good is a head if one does not use it?

CLERK OF THE COURT [*To* JURORS]: Write that down. [JURORS *write with great squeaking of pencils; repeating the words in chorus.*]

ALICE [*aloud to herself*]: I'm glad they do not feel that way about it at home. It would be rather sad for the mothers and fathers of some of the children I know.

KING [*in thundering voice*]: On with the next case!

RABBIT [*blows trumpet.* SOLDIERS *hurry out, returning with the* DUCHESS *carrying pepperbox. Sneezes are heard throughout courtroom while case is being tried.*]

KING: What charge is brought against this prisoner?

RABBIT: It is said, your Majesty, that she peppers her speech with slang.

ALICE: Whoever heard of such a silly statement? One may pepper one's food, but one cannot pepper one's speech.

QUEEN [*calmly*]: One *may*, one *can*, one *does* pepper one's speech! The effect is quite the same as when there is too much pepper in the food, except instead of irritating the mouth and nose, it irritates the ears.

ALICE [*in great distress*]: But you wouldn't execute a person for a little thing like that, would you? Why, in the United States there are *ever* so many boys and girls who use slang, and no one thinks anything about it.

QUEEN [*firmly*]: They *should* think about it. It is a very important matter.

KING [*reading from book*]: "Slang is an expression of weakness and ignorance. It shows that you are not willing to take the time or make the effort to find out the proper method of expressing yourself, or else you are blind to the possibilities of your language." [*Closes book with bang. To the* EXECU-TIONER.] Off with the Duchess' head! Bury the pepperbox! [EXECUTIONER *places* DUCHESS *next to* HATTER *with face to wall. Hurries pepperbox out of Court amid much sneezing.*] Silence! How can I give orders in such a racket? [*To the* RABBIT]: Call the next case.

RABBIT [*blows trumpet.* SOLDIERS *rush out. Return with two prisoners.* RABBIT *reads from scroll*]: Tweedledum and Tweedledee agreed to have a battle for Tweedledum said Tweedledee had spoiled his nice new rattle."

ALICE [*eagerly rushing up to* TWEEDLEDUM *and* TWEEDLE-DEE]: Really and truly, did you fight over such a trifle?

TWEEDLEDUM [*pulling forelock and bowing*]: No, Miss, the rattle didn't have a thing to do with it. That was the reporter's way of writing it up.

ALICE: What was the trouble then?

TWEEDLEDEE [*pulling forelock and bowing*]: I'll explain it. Tweedledum insisted upon using singular subjects with plural verbs.

TWEEDLEDUM: And he [*pointing to* TWEEDLEDEE] insisted upon using plural subjects with singular verbs.

TWEEDLEDEE [*jerking thumb in* TWEEDLEDUM'*s direction*]: So nothing he said agreed—

TWEEDLEDUM: —with anything I said.

QUEEN: The sad part of it was, you both knew better.

TWEEDLEDUM and TWEEDLEDEE [*bowing*]: Yes, your Majesty, but our words got twisted.

KING: Your motto should be, "Watch your speech."

ALICE [*to* KING]: You mean "Watch your step," do you not?

KING [*sternly*]: I mean what I say, or, in other words, I say what I mean. It is more important to watch one's speech than to watch one's step. If one forgets his feet he hurts only himself, but if he forgets his tongue he injures not only himself but others as well.

ALICE [*to* KING]: You have such a curious way of explaining things.

QUEEN [*to* ALICE]: The King's words may be described as wise, but never curious, my dear.

RABBIT [*pointing to* ALICE]: Your Majesty, this creature has repeatedly disturbed my dignity and the dignity of the Court with her irrelevant remarks. I therefore move that the

Court issue an adjudication on this biped, under apprehension.

ALICE [*angrily*]: And I move that the White Rabbit be punished for using such long words. I am sure I don't know what he is talking about. And what is more, I don't believe he does either.

QUEEN: Your point is well taken, Alice.

KING [*looking at* ALICE]: It is said that people who live in glass houses should not throw stones. Your English, Alice, is quite as faulty as the White Rabbit's.

QUEEN [*to* KING]: They are both apprentices, my dear. Every apprentice must learn to know his tools before he can use them well. Let us hope some day Alice and the White Rabbit will become masters. They will then take pride in the beauty and majesty of the English language and learn to choose their words as they choose flowers—because of their affection for them. [*Turning to* KING]: My dear, if I do not put a roast in the oven at once, you will have no dinner. I therefore move that the Court be adjourned.

CLERK OF THE COURT: Jurors remember to put up your slates and powder your wigs!

[*Scraping of chairs; much confusion. The* KING *arises, offers arm to* QUEEN. *The* SOLDIERS *follow holding up trains of* KING *and* QUEEN. *The* JURORS *walk two by two; the* CLERK OF COURT *and the* LORD HIGH EXECUTIONER *bring up the rear of the procession.* ALICE *curtsies to* KING *and* QUEEN. ALICE, *the* RABBIT, *and the condemned subjects are left in Court.*]

ALICE [*claps hands in glee*]: The Executioner has gone! And the Hatter, the Duchess, Tweedledee, and Tweedledum still have their heads! [*The prisoners turn in unison and face* ALICE *at these words.*]

RABBIT [*shakes* ALICE *roughly*]: Of course they have their heads. Who said they wouldn't have their heads? You must be dreaming.

Epilogue

(The epilogue may be given in front of the stage curtain.)

ALICE [*enters with* DINAH *in her arms*]: Dinah, did you hear the impertinent White Rabbit say I had been dreaming? Dreaming, the very idea! [*Pauses.*] Anyway if it was a dream it was the most real dream I ever had. I shall never forget the King and Queen, the Hatter, the Duchess, Tweedledum and Tweedledee, and the White Rabbit of Grammarland. Dinah, you should have been with me. It would have been a real education for you. Even *I* learned a great deal. From now on, I am going to watch your speech and mine most carefully. Let me see! What was the new word you were to add to your vocabulary? You do not remember it? Well, all I have to say, Dinah, is that it is much safer for you to carry that stupid little head of yours around in the U.S.A. than it would be in Grammarland. [*Exit from stage.*]

ALSO AVAILABLE FROM EVERTYPE

Alice's Adventures in Wonderland, 2008

Through the Looking-Glass and What Alice Found There
2009

Wonderland Revisited and the Games Alice Played There
by Keith Sheppard, 2009

A New Alice in the Old Wonderland
by Anna Matlack Richards, 2009

New Adventures of Alice, by John Rae, 2010

Alice's Adventures under Ground, 2009

The Nursery "Alice", 2010

The Hunting of the Snark, 2010

Alice's Adventures in Wonderland,
Retold in words of one Syllable by Mrs J. C. Gorham, 2010

Clara in Blunderland, by Caroline Lewis, 2010

Lost in Blunderland: The further adventures of Clara
by Caroline Lewis, 2010

John Bull's Adventures in the Fiscal Wonderland
by Charles Geake, 2010

The Westminster Alice, by H. H. Munro (Saki), 2010

Alice in Blunderland: An Iridescent Dream
by John Kendrick Bangs, 2010

Rollo in Emblemland, by J. K. Bangs & C. R. Macauley, 2010

Eachtraí Eilíse i dTír na nIontas
Alice in Irish, 2007

Lastall den Scáthán agus a bhFuair Eilís Ann Roimpi
Looking-Glass in Irish, 2009

Alys in Pow an Anethow
Alice in Cornish, 2009

La Aventuroj de Alicio en Mirlando
Alice in Esperanto, 2009

Les Aventures d'Alice au pays des merveilles
Alice in French, 2010

Alice's Abenteuer im Wunderland
Alice in German, 2010

Le Avventure di Alice nel Paese delle Meraviglie
Alice in Italian, 2010

Alicia in Terra Mirabili
Alice in Latin, 2011

Alice ehr Eventuurn in't Wunnerland
Alice in Low German, 2010

Contoyrtyssyn Ealish ayns Çheer ny Yindyssyn
Alice in Manx, 2010

Ailice's Àventurs in Wunnerland
Alice in Scots, 2011

Alices Äventyr i Sagolandet
Alice in Swedish, 2010

Anturiaethau Alys yng Ngwlad Hud
Alice in Welsh, 2010

Lightning Source UK Ltd.
Milton Keynes UK
30 October 2010

162146UK00001B/42/P